Prayer Agents Manual

Jackie Jones Jr.

DEDICATION

To all those individuals who model Colossians 4:2 AMP " Be persistent and devoted to prayer, being alert and focused in your prayer life with an attitude of thanksgiving. I honor you for staying on the wall and standing in the gap as an intercessor. I take this time to share some of my encounters with the Holy spirit as well as my experience in prayer with you as suggestions to help catapult your spirit man to another level.

I want to dedicate this book to my amazing wife, Apostle Jae Jones who has pushed me through with much support, prayer, and encouragement. I love you honey. I could not have done this without you by my side.

CONTENTS

Prayer and Aviation Revelation:

2021 I was on the airplane leaving Chicago heading to San Francisco, CA to support a brother of mine in ministry. The returning aircraft had televisions on the back of every head rest of the seats. The screens gave the passengers the ability to watch movies, listen to music or see two different views of a map that showing the exact place where we were currently traveling and the distance between our destination.

As I looked at the map, I noticed that we departed from California and traveled through Nevada, Idaho, Wyoming, South Dakota, Iowa and into Illinois.

During the 4-hour flight, we crossed a total of 5 states between our departure and arrival as we traveled from the west coast to the Midwest. Including the departure and arrival states there were 7 states in total that were covered during our flight. As an excited passenger but also one of prayer and intercession, I grabbed my phone and took a photo of the screen. What excited me the most was not just seeing states being covered or entered by this aircraft but the image of an airplane with a trail of dotted lines behind it, gave me a visual that what we had crossed left a mark. The line connected us from the departure state into the current state which I was able to see at the time. The screen provided me with information of how high we are by way of altitude, and how much of flight time was left to reach our destination.

Now, of course I must provide you with some revelation from the Almighty God concerning airplanes. The attraction I have to aviation is intense, especially being one who has a natural displeasure of heights. I would like to share what the spirit of the Lord told me:

Prayers that take off from one region and goes to another can travel just as fast, if not faster.
Prayer is like an aircraft! It has a process of taking off and entering the air. Once the airplane reaches a certain altitude in the air, it then passes over many regions. At the appropriate time, the aircraft lands in the state of its intended destination.

What I love about airplanes is everyone is expected to ascend! What do I mean by that? I am so glad you asked. Once all passengers who are assigned to their respective aircrafts board, at the point of take-off, we all ascend together. The only direction for the aircraft to go is up, hence the first word in

aircraft is "air". The purpose in the design of an aircraft is to thrive in the air which means if it were to stay on the ground and operate as a street vehicle, it would be illegal. The aircraft is for the ground temporarily, but the purpose and function of its creation is to dominate in the air.
Prayer Agents, your role is not limited to the ground; but we were created to dominate an entire earth and that includes the air.

Let's keep going, there are many different seats on airplanes:

- ❖ First class
- ❖ Main cabin
- ❖ Coach
- ❖ Economy

Note: some of these classifications differ per airline.

Some passengers paid more for where their preferred seating. This means that, based on the comfort of the passenger, it was preferable to spend more money so that their time in the air could be more satisfying.

There are passengers who paid for checked baggage while others receive it free of charge for their travel. Regardless of the class chosen for the flight or the cost paid, all passengers are on the same plane headed to the same destination. At the end of the flight, all passengers will land in the same destination to disembark.

Here's another observation consider regarding prayer, intercession, and airplanes:
When the seatbelt sign comes on, it aligns those on the aircraft while in the air.
The seatbelt sign, which lights up during the flight, serves as an indicator for passengers to comply with safety measures. It is for protection which appears when there is a lot of turbulence or if the plane is still ascending to its expected altitude. Once we reach a certain height in the air, at the discretion of the pilot, the seatbelt can be temporarily removed. As we prepare for landing, the seatbelt sign comes on again, and we unite in spirit to prepare for a safe landing.

Final part of this revelation is this there must be equal weight distribution on the plane, so that we are evenly balanced. The aircraft carries a specific amount of luggage in addition to the passengers.

Let's look at this from a prayer and intercession place of unity in the spirit.

We all come into this space because we need God (destination)

Question: Was showing up to prayer the final answer or destination? Saying, "I showed up so that automatically gets me to Him," should not be a factor in the minds of kings and priests.

Does the fact that you paid money, booked a flight, and boarded the plane guarantees that you're going to take off, reach the air and get to your destination?

Disclaimer as I prepare you for the journey into THE GLORY:
1.   YOUR BOARDING PASS VALIDATES that you have a seat on the plane!
2.   YOUR involvement and engagement are vital on this journey; you didn't come to this plane to sit there and NOT TAKE OFF.
3.   YOUR expectation should always not only be for yourself but for everyone involved.

Prayer Agents, we are time travelers who engage with our father in prayer and intercession causing every region and territory to be covered. Isaiah 6:2-3 GW "2 Angels [a] were standing above him. Each had six wings: With two they covered their faces, with two they covered their feet, and with two they flew. ³ They called to each other and said,

"Holy, holy, holy is the Lord of Armies!
The whole earth is filled with his glory."

The whole earth is filled with the glory of the Lord, which means as we activate our posture of prayer and intercession, and He responds, the earth shall be filled to its capacity with GLORY.

As you dive into this Prayer Agents Manual, language will be imparted that will serve as weaponry for every assigned king and priest who dominates the earth against the adversaries of this world.

1 AGENTS OF PRAYER

I have been asked over the last few years, "What is a Prayer Agent" and what do they do? In my mind, I initially wanted to direct everyone who asked that question to my first book which is titled "Prayer Agents". However, over time, I realized that the world needs a clearer explanation of who prayer agents are and how one can enlist.

When my book was released August 2020, the title of Prayer Agent was often diminished from plural to singular. As I would go out to minister, attend gatherings or any event, I would be referenced as "THE PRAYER AGENT". Little did the people know, I really disliked being identified in that manner because my pursuit was not to be seen as one who does the work alone, but rather as one who authorizes and deputizes others to this call of prayer and intercession. I found it almost belittling and diminishing of my endeavor. Here me out, those of us who understand our call to prayer and intercession already know that this can feel lonely. Intercession is a burdened place where God places this burden on you to cry out until He releases it from you. It can be a lonely road as an intercessor. It's even more burdensome when you not only feel the weight of it but also see that others are not joining you in prayer. Prayers that need to be prayed are NOT being released. People whom God is calling to pray and intercede are running away from the call. Individuals you have watched labor in prayer and intercession are falling away and deciding they just don't care to do so anymore. It's tough on the prayer and intercession community. Jesus said "men ought to always pray" Luke 18:1, but I'm afraid that there is a great percentage of men who chooses to say "if I pray, I pray", "I'll leave it to others and reap the benefits of it all". OH yeah, it's tough. Hearing repeatedly that I, Jackie Jones Jr, is "THE PRAYER AGENT", I said to myself, I can either get upset about it or educate and empower people on the knowledge, definition, and charge for Prayer Agents in the earth.

Prayer Agents is a community of believers in Jesus Christ who understand the vitality of prayer and intercession in the earth. Prayer agents are individuals with many spiritual gifts and remain true to the notion that every gift from God is effective only through prayer and intercession.

I remember when I began my classical dance training, and I was drawn to jazz technique heavily.

Watching the dancers in the studio move to upbeat music, with grand battement (high kicks), and going from triple pirouettes to a Jete (turn to a leap), I was fascinated by the fast-paced nature of the class and how the dancers used so much of their bodies to accomplish the steps in so little time. I recall saying to myself, "I want to get there one day and that one day is NOW". Boy, I mean I was craving that clean execution of movement and to be in that class. It was my freshman year at Columbia College Chicago which marked the start of my professional dance training. The class I would faithfully watch after my classes ended, was jazz level ¾, an upper-level advanced class. I didn't care how advanced it was; all I knew was I WANTED TO BE IN THERE. My dance counselor at the time said to me, "Jackie, I know you want to do Jazz, but you need Ballet as your foundation, and you have to start and the beginning level." I was upset and disappointed because my thoughts on ballet were not positive. The idea of being in a class with a live pianist playing slow songs, and wearing leotards, tights, and ballet shoes did not sit well with me. For two semesters, I avoided ballet and took more contemporary technique classes. However, I was continually directed by each instructor that I need ballet. You see, ballet is the core value and basis of all movement. It teaches you how to become one with your core (center), and how to focus. Ballet instills discipline and helps you understand the anatomy of the body.

Here I was, wanting to avoid the basics of all movement to get to a fast-paced, entertaining element of dance, while ignoring the fact that you can't execute without the basics. Yes, you can learn steps and mimic the leaps, but it won't be movement with true understanding. Once you grasp it, how do you grow from it? How do you maintain what you have learned? I would have found myself constantly trying to find the answer without going through the proper formula it takes to get the right answer. Not just the right answer, but a healthier conclusion.

Saints, it was difficult, but I found myself taking this beginning ballet class. It was in this class where my insecurities, failures, and weaknesses were exposed, as I was the student who just couldn't seem to get anything right. I had always believed within myself that I excelled at anything I put my mind to. I was accustomed to winning awards, trophies, certificates for vocal performances in high school and middle school. Now, I found myself in a class where all of that seemed to be tearing me down, or so I thought. However, ballet was building me up while stripping away every ounce of pride and control within me. My goal was to reach that advanced jazz level, so I had to start by committing to do the work.

After giving it my all, I advanced from beginning ballet to ballet level 2/3. Yes, I skipped Ballet 1 and jumped to a higher level because I put in the work and applied the principles of movement. After two semesters of hard work, I finally made it to advanced jazz class and became one of the top students in the class. Want to know what I did differently? I attended beginning ballet, Ballet level 2/3, and never stopped sitting outside of that advanced jazz class. As I applied the basics from beginning ballet while observing the advanced jazz class, I would go home and practice for 3-4 hours a day. Once I enrolled in advanced jazz, I was ready. I learned the terminology, the stretches, every pique, pirouette, and turn there was to perfection.

I wanted to share my experience for two reasons. First, because it was one of my greatest success stories in my life, and secondly, because we must understand that we all have a gift and ability within us, but it is only at its greatest when you apply the basics and go back to home base. You may be a gifted musician, singer, author, athlete, and it's all God-given, but without prayer and intercession those gifts are not as effective. Hear me say "not as effective". The gift works, and it will make an impact, but for it to have longevity and wider impact, apply prayer and intercession to it consistently, and oh my Lord, you will see the hand of the Lord move like never before.

When I think of Prayer Agents, I envision community. I see the spirit of unity and oneness in God. As I began to share my dance experience, I realized that the terminology used to describe certain movements might not be understood by everyone who reads this manual. This is because the writing is not limited to dancers alone but to anyone who decides to engage with this manual. Dancers understand terms like "grand battement" whereas non-dancers may require more details and explanation. The artistic community comprehends the language of the arts, which is why you can put singers, dancers, musicians, and painters in one room and the creativity that flows would be astounding. Artists understand one another because creatives possess vivid imaginations and expressions that others may not comprehend, but they benefit from what we, as creatives and artists, produce.

This is why God led me to release the term "Prayer Agents". It will be a community of people understand prayer and intercession. Yes, it is a gift, but there is more to it than just a "gift", "anointing", or something "supernatural". We understand as Prayer Agents that it's about making impact on the earth that represents the kingdom of God WELL.

The book centered around the birthing of new terminology that would empower the saints of God to be more than just prayer warriors and intercessors, but to be more versed in the spiritual things of God through prayer and intercession, if that makes sense. Prayer Agents is a defining category or job title description for what we do in the realm of the spirit and is not limited to one way of communicating with God. Prayer and Intercession do not have a limit but do have various ranks, positions, assignments, and much more set to make greater impacts in the earth with the support of Heaven.

My reasoning for releasing the title "Prayer Agents" into the earth was not to create a trending name that will look good on apparel or to change the biblical terminology or identity that describes one who prays. The title was given to me through the Holy Ghost to emphasize specific tasks that come along with prayer and intercession, which charges the believer to think outside the box.

Just as every community has a bonding place that

unites them, so does prayer and intercession. What makes one qualified to be a Prayer Agent? Simple answer, "one who is saved by grace through faith" (Ephesians 2:8), which means you are a believer of Jesus Christ. Once you have accepted Jesus Christ into your heart, you have been granted the gift of prayer and intercession. There is an instant access that comes to you from God that gives you permission to communicate with Him according to His word. Wow wow wow! Therefore, the prayer agents community is accessible to you providing language, culture, development, instruction, teaching and revelation on how to use your gift to make an impact in this world.

Hear me, we do not pray and intercede for ourselves the entire time. Prayer and intercession were not created for selfish gain but it was created and granted to us by God for us to pray His divine will for THE EARTH. The Bible says in Psalms 24:1a GW "The earth and everything it contains are the Lord's. The world and all who live in it are his."

Listen to the order. The earth is the Lord's. In the beginning, God created the heavens and the earth. Already, the first target of prayer and intercession IS THE EARTH! Not money, not our bills, not even people. It is to pray for God's Will to be done IN

THE EARTH as it is in Heaven.

Let's delve deeper in scripture: Here are four tiers that we should be praying for consistently:

- ❖ The heavens
- ❖ The earth
- ❖ The world
- ❖ The people

Scripture references:
Romans 8:19 KJV "¹⁹ For the earnest expectation of the creature waiteth for the manifestation of the sons of God.

Genesis 1:1 KJV "In the beginning God created the heavens and the earth."

Matthew 6: 10 KJV "Thy kingdom come they will be done in earth as it is in heaven.

Why are we praying for the heavens? It is in the heavens where the will of God is already manifested. Psalms 115:3 KJV "But our God is in the heavens: he hath done whatsoever he hath pleased. VERSE 16: The heaven, even the heavens, are the Lord's: but the earth hath he given to the children of men.

By way of the word of God, we understand that our God created the heavens, He lives above the heavens, and He orchestrates, dominates, and controls the heavens. When we pray to heaven, we are seeking instruction, information, and insight into what we need to cover on the earth. We are seeking the WILL of God that has been established in the heavens to be established here on earth. The heavens are the domain of God. We don't have authority to tell the heavens what to do, but we can ask for divine assistance in our pursuit for God to be revealed here on earth.

Isaiah 64: 1 KJV "Oh that thou wouldest rend the heavens, that thou wouldest come down, that the mountains might flow down at thy presence."

This is a place of prayer as we request that God's Will be made known on earth by coming through the heavens into the earth by way of His spirit. My God! This is powerful! We make a request for the heavens to be opened. The heavens become open through our prayer and intercession but also through our giving.

Malachi 3:10 KJV:
10 Bring ye all the tithes into the storehouse, that there may be meat in mine house, and prove me now herewith, saith the Lord of hosts, if I will not

open you the windows of heaven, and pour you out a blessing, that there shall not be room enough to receive it.

Key terms if I will not OPEN YOU…in other words, God is saying by way of offering, giving, and obedience, I will open you the windows of heaven. As we seek the father and seek for the heavens, THINGS OPEN!

Why are we praying for the earth? The earth was the next point of creation in Genesis 1:1 In the beginning God created the heaven and the earth.

The heaven is for Him, the earth is for man. The earth is the created place in which all things exist. The earth is our gift from God to us as His children. We dominate and rule on earth. Our job as sons, kings and priests is to ensure that the creation, known as earth, always match what is in heaven. We are to pray and intercede for the earth until it has no blemishes, no tarnished looks, but emulates what's happening where our Father resides.

Satan was banned from heaven but not from earth. He was not bound to hell just as God is not bound to heaven. The earth is the access point for both to function. The difference is God came in the form of flesh into the earth granting Him oneness with the earth to do as He pleases. He had the power to run and rule in what He created. Satan could enter the earth but not dominate the earth. He needed access to get in to corrupt it and seek to dominate who he can and what he can, but the earth will never be under his rulership or control. He didn't die for the world therefore he can't own the world. Blood was shed by Jesus Christ and covered the earth which grants Him permission to legislate in it.

Satan being banned from heaven did not ban him from the garden. The garden was an access point to become legal in the earth which ultimately was giving him a thought pattern that he could find a way to dominate and rule what God created. He was seeking to infiltrate the plan of God for the future.

Why did Satan want access in the garden? Why did he come for Eve which is the rib Adam gave up unconsciously? He did not give up his rib by choice and was not aware that something was being removed from him that would bless him for the rest of his life. Satan, in the form of a serpent, came to Eve but not Adam. However, Adam became aware and connected to the sin through what came out of him (woman).

Satan needed more people to manipulate and find a

way to rule and control. The third of angels that went with him when he was kicked out of heaven was the start of rulership, but he desired more.

Satan's plan was to find a way to infiltrate the systems of the world and ultimately dominate them all by any means necessary. He's not after you alone but what you gave up! Whatever you give up, he wants to find a way into that thing to hold you hostage and dominate you.

Job 1:6-7 GW "6 One day when the sons of God came to stand in front of the Lord, Satan the Accuser came along with them.
7 The Lord asked Satan, "Where have you come from?"
Satan answered the Lord, "From wandering all over the earth."

I Peter 5:8 KJV
Be sober, be vigilant; because your adversary the devil, as a roaring lion, walketh about, seeking whom he may devour:

This is the tactic of Satan, who walks the earth in search of his next Eve. Who will engage with him? Who will listen to him? Who will accept his cunning words and believe in him, so that he can find a way to destroy? He desires the earth as his own, which ultimately is his goal for souls. However, Satan knows he will never obtain the earth. What he is aiming for is payback with God for casting him out of heaven and stripping him of his rights, while also harboring hatred for the children of men who have been given authority to dominate and rule. If he can take the earth by storm and manipulate as many people as possible before its end, then he has accomplished his objective. Satan is after the earth to create a shortage in the kingdom of God. He wants to fill up hell with as many souls as possible in an effort to make God's creation appear pointless devoid of purpose. It's almost as if he aims to depict God as a liar and to make Him regret creating the earth, while simultaneously attempting to make God regret casting Satan out.

Genesis 6: 5-8-GW "[5] The Lord saw how evil humans had become on the earth. All day long their deepest thoughts were nothing but evil. [6] The Lord was sorry that he had made humans on the earth, and he was heartbroken. [7] So he said, "I will wipe off the face of the earth these humans that I created. I will wipe out not only humans, but also domestic animals, crawling animals, and birds. I'm sorry that I made them." [8] But the Lord was pleased with Noah.

Here is what the enemy would love to bring to the

attention of God as a reminder that what He created doesn't deserve to remain on earth. Oh, but thank God for the favor shown to a man named Noah. It was one man who interrupted what should have been the destruction of all created beings on earth. I believe this is why the Lord has not destroyed the earth, and it's because of His favored intercessors. Glory!

It's indeed a war between good and evil. We must pray for the earth to submit totally to God, as it was created to do and be.

Satan's goal is to steal, kill and destroy as many souls as possible. The more souls he possesses, the greater the count for the kingdom of darkness. If given access to one's heart, soul, mind, and body, he can then find his way to dominate and control them. The more souls he eradicates from the earth, the more difficult it becomes for the kingdom of God to prevail. He wants to wipe out the earth and everything inside of it until there is nothing left for God to use. If he cannot eradicate the creation known as earth, he then desires to leave the earth empty so that no one remains.

Why do we pray for the world? What is the world? The world is what enables the earth to function.

For example, all land with dirt is not automatically a garden. What transforms the land turn into a garden is what has been planted in the soil through seeds and how it is cultivated and tended to. Planting seeds in the soil causes them to grow, resulting in a garden. The earth was created by God to sustain the world and its inhabitants, reflecting the original intent of creation.

Jesus died and shed blood for the lost so they can be found. He died so that the world could repent and receive redemption and reconciliation to Him. This includes the unsaved men and women but also everything that enables the earth to function.

The systems we live and function in:
1. Healthcare and medical
2. Business
3. Religion
4. Education
5. Arts and entertainment
6. Media
7. Family
8. Government

It is our assignment and charge as prayer agents to reign and rule over the systems of the world until they submit to Jesus Christ.

Why do we pray for the people? It's simple: people are the access point to good or evil. Listen to what happened with Adam and Eve, in Genesis 2:25 KJV "And they were both naked, the man and his wife, and were not ashamed."

Living in the garden as husband and wife while being in the presence of God all day and all night, was perfection for Adam and Eve. They were living in a place where there was no definition for sin or nakedness to which they were exposed to.

Look at Genesis 3: 6-11 KJV

6 And when the woman saw that the tree was good for food, and that it was pleasant to the eyes, and a tree to be desired to make one wise, she took of the fruit thereof, and did eat, and gave also unto her husband with her; and he did eat.
7 And the eyes of them both were opened, and they knew that they were naked; and they sewed fig leaves together and made themselves aprons.
8 And they heard the voice of the Lord God walking in the garden in the cool of the day: and Adam and his wife hid themselves from the presence of the Lord God amongst the trees of the garden.

9 And the Lord God called unto Adam, and said unto him, Where art thou?

10 And he said, I heard thy voice in the garden, and I was afraid, because I was naked; and I hid myself.

11 And he said, Who told thee that thou wast naked? Hast thou eaten of the tree, whereof I commanded thee that thou shouldest not eat?

The change occurred from being naked and unashamed to heeding an illegitimate voice, which caused them to see themselves as something shameful. The term "naked" was normal in Genesis 2:25, but after they sinned, the word 'naked' became associated with shame. How did Adam learn that? Where did that come from?

Think about newborn babies entering the world: innocent, unknowledgeable, and unbothered about life. Newborns are under the care of an adult or guardian who is responsible for feeding them, changing diapers, rocking them to sleep and nurturing them to their next phase of life. Babies have the luxury of entering the world carefree, laughing when they want to laugh, cry when they want to cry, and eating when they want. Everything is great until, at some point in their developmental stages of life, understanding comes into play. When babies reach the toddler stage and begin to walk, they start hearing things like 'you can't touch this', or 'you can't eat that', and the restrictions go on and on because what was once carefree now has to be handled differently. Babies start to become curious about the new restrictions placed on them, which may cause them to adapt or rebel. As growth continues to happen, there are more rules, more restrictions, more teachings, and it just keeps going. Life starts getting more confusing in a sense, as what is being taught at home may differ from what society and educational system teaches. Life progresses further, and it gets to a place where, once a baby, toddler, child, to youth and teens, individuals formulate opinions, ideas, and judgments on everything.

I am saying all of this because as prayer agents, we need to pray and intercede for all people. In the world, there are so many people who DO NOT KNOW that there is a Savior. Many are listening to these serpents talking them out of the presence of God so that they can enter their lives and disconnect them from their original position or posture. We were created to be in His presence and understand His plan. However, with many loud voices in the earth dominating airwaves, social media platforms, the music and arts industry, and more, it becomes challenging to decipher between what God is REALLY saying to the church versus the loud opinions of others in the earth using the name of Jesus Christ as their support.

Opinions of God, His word, His ways, and His character presented to the world through social media outlets are confusing and oftentimes lure us into an intriguing, thought-provoking mindset, causing us to consider disowning everything we know about God. It's rough!!!!!

What we believed to be right about God, based upon opposing viewpoints from others, can sometimes make our beliefs questionable. Who we thought God was to us is now up for grabs because the information presented seems so RIGHT that there's no need to research it for ourselves. We just go with it. This has been the current state for quite a few people in the world.

Many great books have been published, and many podcasts and audiobooks have been released with great content and exquisite use of scripture, but some carry a spirit of division. The spirit of confusion and division, with an intent to lure the saints away from the true gospel of Jesus Christ, is on the horizon. Fabrications of the Bible and misrepresentation of our Lord is on the rise, and they are set to kill the knowledge of truth in generations. But as we step up as prayer agents and combat the lies of the enemy, we will see God move in the earth, the world, and for His people.

2 HOW PRAYER AGENTS IMPACT THE EARTH

My introduction to the terminology and language of prayer and intercession was through the book titled 'Prayer Agents: Impacting the World for the Kingdom of God'. The book provided a definition of the title/name "Prayer Agent" in acronym form, helping the reader understand how we function in the earth. Here is a brief reminder:

Praying and Prophesying
Releasing
Activating
Yielding
Empowering
Renewing
Aligning
Governing
Establishing
Navigating
Trailblazing

The inspiration behind Prayer Agents started with my fascination with murder mysteries and crime-solving, including books, movies, and television series. I've always been captivated by watching men and women who boldly pursue criminals to find out the "why" behind their crimes. As a child, I was obsessed with cartoons like Scooby -Doo, Where in the World is Carmen San Diego, and Inspector Gadget. I would spend hours watching Scooby-Doo, trying to discover who the monster was before the end of the show. Sometimes I could figure it out, and other times I was shocked along with the rest of the gang. Carmen San Diego was a smooth criminal in more ways than one. Sometimes the team would find her, and just before they capture her, she would disappear into thin air or have some clever way of escaping. Inspector Gadget may not have been the smartest, but between Penny and the dog, the three of them would apprehend the criminal.

As an adult, I'm mesmerized by crime-solving cases, cold case files, and the work done by those in CSI and the criminal justice system to solve crimes. The process of working backward from a homicide to uncover the answers needed to solve the crime is intriguing. The discovery starts at the end, rather than the beginning, and depending on whether the perpetrator is quickly apprehended or still at large, investigators must move swiftly. If the criminal is still at large, a plan must be quickly devised to capture them before they commit another crime. If the criminal has been apprehended, time must be spent (whether they are dead or alive), to uncover the motive behind the crime.

The research involved in determining motive, identifying involved parties, examining weapons, analyzing the crime scene, reviewing phone records, and exploring the history of the criminal(s) and victim(s) history can be overwhelming. Deciphering the motive, whether pure or unintentional, can take some time. However, it doesn't stop these investigators from doing their job and seeking justice for the sake of the family, the deceased, and the city where they as assigned. You hear this?

There is so much more I can say, but this is how I see Prayer Agents. We are like crime scene investigators because we operate on the earth. We are not limited to a city, region, territory, demographic of people but cover the ENTIRE EARTH.

For instance, while we know that crime exists, death occurs, and murders happen, what we don't initially is why it happened, who did it and the motive behind it. Nor are we fully aware of the background history of the perpetrator or the victim. We take the time to investigate the crime(s) that occur frequently. We delve into research, examining every person and everything connected to them. We search for evidence, looking for foul play, and scrutinizing every key player and those connected to the intended target.

It's the same with prayer and intercession. We know the enemy comes to steal, kill, and destroy, but in his pursuit of that, we need to identify targets and find answers. Get to him or stop him before his plan prevails. Cover the people before they become victimized.

God was a crime scene investigator in Genesis 4:8-10 GW "[8] Cain talked to his brother Abel. Later, when they were in the fields, Cain attacked his brother Abel and killed him.

[9] The Lord asked Cain, "Where is your brother Abel?"

"I don't know," he answered. "Am I supposed to take care of my brother?"

[10] The Lord asked, "What have you done? Your brother's blood is crying out to me from the ground.

Here we see God speaking to Cain concerning the blood that cries out from the ground, which is

Abel's. The interrogation begins, and through Cain's response, God grants punishment.

As we pray and intercede for the earth, the world, and the people, we must research our adversary and what he has infiltrated in our earth. We need to identify what is happening frequently and where it is becoming a trend. For instance, if we are witnessing frequent occurrences of child abductions, let's research the spirit behind it and which cities are most affected. If gun violence and mass school shootings are prevalent, let's map out the cities and states where they occur the most. This knowledge helps us target these issues in prayer and intercession.

Our assignment never ceases until the earth looks resembles the heavens. This means the community of prayer agents is needed and necessary throughout the earth. Hear me, Prayer Agents is not for Jackie Jones Jr. alonen but an agency and community of people who will proclaim these words, "I am an Agent of Prayer, and I am taking back the earth with consistent prayer and intercession".

Prayer Agents save lives!
Prayer Agents save communities!
Prayer Agents save churches!
Prayer Agents save families!

Let's go up Prayer Agents! We have some crimes to solve and some opposing criminals to banish from the earth IN THE NAME OF JESUS CHRIST!

3 HOW TO LEAD CORPORATE PRAYER (ENGAGING WITH GOD IN PERSONAL PRAYER)

It is imperative that we understand effective corporate prayer cannot occur without personal prayer. Often, I've been asked how to overcome the spirit of fear associated with praying openly or corporately.

The key is simple, although it can be multifaceted in its explanation: if I cultivate prayer confidence with God in private then, what I do openly is simply the performance of my rehearsal. In other words, I am merely displaying and inviting the room into what I consistently do with God in private.

There were times when I would cook a dish and share it on my social media platform. While I enjoyed the taste at home or critiqued what I could have done better, others would comment and ask if they could have some. Reluctant to share, I'd respond with things like "Well I cooked enough for me", or "you should have come over". In my mind, I told myself that while it might be good enough for me, it might not be well-received by others. Perhaps the recipe I followed appealed to me but not to others. Maybe the way I put sauce on the food wouldn't please someone else. Therefore, I often chose not to share anything I cooked because I felt it wouldn't be appreciated.

One Christmas, my family gathered at my home, and I decided to prepare the food for dinner. I stayed up all night, ensuring that I followed the recipe and cooked the food the way I would for myself. To my surprise, many of the dishes I prepared were eagerly transferred to their plates, and by the end of dinner, there was hardly any room for seconds or leftovers. I remember thinking to myself, "You spent time perfecting your recipe, Jackie, and you received the response from your guests that you would give yourself in private."

This experience taught me the importance of investing time and effort into what matters, whether it's' cooking for loved ones or spending time what God. Just as I showed up and gave my best in cooking for my family, I encourage you to be timely in your pursuit of spending time with God. Show up, be present, stay committed, and be true to who you are as a prayer agent. We stand on the wall and will not come down from that position until God has manifested His presence in the earth.

Now, let's delve deeper as I share some experiences

that will support engaging with God in personal prayer and offer tips for leading corporate prayer.

I once attended a service that was advertised as "Night of the Miraculous." The title alone excited me because anything geared towards the miraculous power of God indicates an atmosphere where He can demonstrate His power. However, it's important to note that whatever we label our services, gatherings, conferences, workshops should be led by the spirit of God. Words have power, so whatever is declared in the earth will also attract the spirit associated with it. If we lack the spiritual capacity to harbor and release what we label our service, it may not live up to its expectations.

This is why many times we attend these gatherings with high expectations but are left disappointed because the advertised does not occur as expected. When a name or title is published and the spirit assigned to that title is released, we see manifestation. When we call on the name of Jesus in spirit and in truth and utilize the power within us that connects to His name, we gain His presence.

However, if there's unbelief present, the power of God may not manifest as expected. We must seek wise counsel from The Father and label our gatherings appropriately based on our current spiritual capacity or where we desire to reach. If we aim to reach a place beyond our current capacity, then we need the momentum and drive to labor in prayer and intercession for that desired outcome.

In other words, If I advertise a healing service but the spiritual atmosphere within my local assembly is primarily focused on a shout and dance with no genuine belief in the healing power of God, then our prayers as intercessory prayers need to be directed appropriately. Our prayers should target not only the attendees of the healing service but also those within the congregation who are tasked with releasing the healing anointing. Hear me Prayer Agents, there are many services, conferences, workshops that are opened to the public that may be a misrepresentation of the power of Jesus Christ. The advertisement says one thing, but the capacity of the host is another. God speaks to His leaders (i.e. senior pastors and visionaries), but as Prayer Agents we are to push them in the spirit that what they produce remains aligned with the timing and spirit of God.

Look at Simon in Acts 8:9-13 GW "⁹ A man named Simon lived in that city. He amazed the people of Samaria with his practice of magic. He claimed that he was great. ¹⁰ Everyone from children to adults paid attention to him. They said, "This man is the power of God, and that power is called great." [11] They paid attention to Simon because he had amazed them for a long time with his practice of magic. [12] However, when Philip spread the Good News about God's kingdom and the one named Jesus Christ, men and women believed him and were baptized. [13] Even Simon believed, and after he was baptized, he became devoted to Philip. Simon was amazed to see the miracles and impressive things that were happening.

Simon was possibly hosting revivals, drawing larger crowds each time. The people attending was mesmerized by the workings of Simon so much that he was referred to as the great power of God. Many of these people attending could have seen Simon as one who is anointed because he performed well, and his flyers may have been super attractive. However, what he was doing was summoning evil spirits into every gathering. It took for Phillip, a man filled with the Holy Spirit, to come in the name of Jesus Christ to deliver and convert these people. All it took was for Phillip to come one time in the right spirit and deliverance, healing, and more broke out in Samaria.

As it pertains to hosting these spiritual gatherings some lack maturity in the spirit, or sufficient knowledge and tend to confuse longevity, large crowds, and large fiscal budgets as indicators of authority in the kingdom. Therefore, as Prayer Agents, we MUST pray for the spirit of maturity to be imparted and revealed to God's people. A few ways to execute a healing service is to release healing scriptures, preach healing sermons, teach on healing principles, and bathe the house under an atmosphere of healing.

There is a preparation involved with a titled service given by God especially if you have allotted time to do so.

If the healing service is scheduled for Sunday, then starting as early as Monday night, the intercessors of the house should begin to make preparations for the atmosphere of healing. God responds to what has been released through prayer, and the capacity of the house to experience a healing move hinges on the unity of faith and the consistency of prayer. Therefore, daily intercession is essential to pave the way for God's healing presence to manifest during the service."

We must remember that false advertisement turns people away which can lead to lack of support and trust from consumers or clientele if we are speaking from a business perspective. Think about this, if a business advertises a 9am opening, and customers arrive at 8:55am and the lights are completely off inside of the building, it is perceived that more time is needed. When 9am gets here and the condition is still the same, it can become slightly alarming. As time progresses to about 9:05-9:10am customers may feel prompted to either call the business directly, knock on the door or decide to seek out another business for their needs because the timing of advertisement proves to be inaccurate.

True Experience: Time of service

There is nothing like having the intention to accomplish a task, project, assignment, or needing to retrieve something and the time is not honored by others. It can be frustrating when you need something done in a timeframe which you have mapped out so perfectly and then distraction comes. As one who prides himself in being organized, strategic and administrative in all areas, nothing makes me more upset than setting a plan of action, only to have it derailed by distractions or interruptions.

One day, as I was preparing to head to work for a shift starting at 11 am, I aimed to leave home earlier than usual to run some last-minute errands before clocking in. Preparing for a photoshoot early the next day, I only had time before work to get some last-minute errands done in efforts to arrive on time. Before leaving, I diligently input the name and address of the place I needed to visit into my GPS, ensuring that I would arrive with ample time to complete what I needed to do. Upon reaching the location, which was just a short 3-minute drive from my workplace and was supposed to open at 10 am according to their website and signage, I found the doors still locked. There was an advertisement on the door, windows, and the awning outside, and there was even an updated hours of operation sign intentionally posted on the front door, suggesting some of the hours had changed from what's plastered all over the building. I read the sign, and it stated that certain days of the week hours were later than advertised, but on this day, it was set to open at 10am. I waited patiently outside for 10mins prior to the open time and as time passed, I noticed it was 3 mins after 10am and it had not opened. Therefore, I called the business. A lady answered the phone, and I politely asked her "Ma'am what time do you open today?" She replied "11am", I said, "Well, it's advertised all over the building and on your updated hours of operation signage that you open at 10am." She replied in a very nonchalant and non-empathetic tone, "No, it's 11am". Hesitantly, as I ended the called, I said to myself, so am I just to accept the fact that what you said, you're not honoring, and you have NO explanation as to why you aren't opening up at the time YOU stated?" I was bothered because I made an intentional effort to get here for a service that I cannot receive at this time. Now, I have to adjust my day and come back again at their convenience when they decide to open and receive the service I need.

As a business owner, the focus should be on providing accurate information so that the customers who are coming into your establishment can provide consistent funding to keep your business functioning WHILE you provide them the requested service(s). I hope you are catching what I am saying both in the natural and spiritual sense. This experience shifted my day completely, but what hit me the most was the additional time spent in my commute to get here ON TIME to receive the service I really needed; the facility was not open to receive me. JESUS MY LORD! I came because you advertised that you would welcome me in at 10am, so I arrived at 9:50am in anticipation of getting service, and you were closed. When I call you, there is no empathy, no apology, no explanation, just "I'm closed so come back when we open an hour later," and that is not convenient for me.

JESUS! Listen to what the spirit of the Lord says in this message. Here is why time is so important and what we commit to God means so much to Him.

We say we are going to pray, and we set up time for Him that we do not always honor. We provide Him with no explanation or excuse but are so dismissive to Him. He's coming to YOUR HOUSE based upon your plethora of services that you offer Him. However, when He arrives at your establishment its closed at the time you say you're open to receive Him.

Think about Sundays- how we come to the house of worship and it's an "open shop" that day. Oh, we are singing, dancing, rejoicing, praising, making all declarations about the Lord, and speaking over our week etc. As the week progresses, what occurred Sunday gets lost, and here comes the Lord ready to move upon the same people who were open, only to find they are all closed. There is no access for Him. There is no room for Him. He can't flow, move, breathe, activate, or fulfill all the things that YOU DECLARED OUT OF YOUR MOUTH.

Let's revisit my experience. So, as the day progressed, and it was time for my lunch, I decided to return to the place that was closed to see if I could receive service. I walked inside, and the lady who greeted me at the door said to me "I don't have any time slots available right now, can you come back later?" With disappointment again, I had to leave the space because now the service I needed from the business that was now open was not available for me.

Can you imagine how God is feeling when He continues to come to the people who are HIS and they say to Him, "Well you can't come back now cause SOMEONE or SOMETHING ELSE has filled up the space."

Should I or could I have made an appointment for this service? Absolutely I could have, but this same place accepted walk-ins which was also made known through their advertisement. Whew, my God.

The point I am referring to is not just the angle of time being wasted, but I showed up to receive service from a specific business that only specialized in the exact service I needed, and what was advertised was incorrect.

When the people attend service, they are expecting to receive what they came for and not feel cheated. Who wants to attend an advertised gospel choir concert only to arrive and find it's a panel discussion without any form of music? One would feel cheated and bamboozled.

Back to my original thought regarding the miracle

prayer service. It was minutes before the service started, and the seats were filled with people. The saints were talking low, some of the saints were praying, it was a mixed atmosphere. A man approached the stage talking rather softly into the microphone and immediately started to speak in his heavenly language. The people in the room were looking, most are sitting, some were standing but the hand claps were few, and the engagement of the people was very limited in this packed-out room. He proceeded into what I believe was prayer, and the usage of vocabulary words was very extensive, which made it challenging to follow, even for me. He continued to pray and then told the people to yell, scream, travail, but the people were quite confused as to what was going on. I admit, I was even thrown for a loop as to where I engage at this moment.

The prayer carried on for quite some time until the next part of the service. Although the prayer moment lasted only a few minutes, it felt like an hour.

I learned something in that moment that remains dear to my heart as a prayer leader. We must understand that when we gather people to enter a place of prayer, every culture is different. There are houses that are deeply rooted in prayer and intercession, where the moment you step to the microphone and pray in your heavenly language, they can take off with you. There are some houses where you begin to express what is about to occur, and they come along with you. There are houses where you literally must coach them by setting up the journey ahead of time, engaging and welcoming them in like a kindergarten class, and eventually, they will get with you. Then there are those that, no matter what you do, how skilled you are, the house is NOT going with you anywhere. Those kinds of houses are possibly robotic, commercialized, and ready to go to the next part of service. Prayer is only a space filler and seems like the right religious thing to do. MY GOD TODAY.

I want to elaborate on Prayer being just a space filler before I move on to my next thought. Prayer IS NOT meant to fill a space in a service. If that becomes the focus of prayer in our local assemblies, then we as a church are in trouble. Do not use prayer to take up time to connect one part of the service to the next if it's not going to be a true place of seeking. Hear me out, we can pray 4-6 times in a service, but if the program remains the same before and after and there is not a real pursuit for God to manifest, then take it off the program.

I would receive invitations to come and minister, and some would say "Pastor Jackie, I want you to be a Firestarter, or I want you to lead 5 minutes of prayer before the singer comes". I would ask them questions like, how long will the singer be up? How long will others minister in the service? I would then ask them what is the purpose of my prayer? What is the target or focus? Many times, I would not get answers, or I would get the "I don't have a target or focus, we just want prayer". Now, before you all judge me let me explain. When we book a guest preacher, we have a focus and target. When we book a singer, we have a focus and target. Oh, but when it's time for the intercessor who breaks the ground so that the singer and preacher can flow under an open heaven, we get time restraints, no direction on our prayer target and focus and in most cases are not treated as a "guest" in your service. I am not saying that the prayer must be a certain length of time to be deemed effective. What I am saying is that we, as intercessors DO NOT PRAY TO FILL A SPACE ON YOUR PROGRAM AND SERVICE. We pray and intercede to reach God and break ground. Plan your service accordingly when you invite us.

Now, I would like to look at this from another angle, which states that intercessors make up the hedge and fill in the gap:
Ezekiel 22:30 KJV
"And I sought for a man among them, that should make up the hedge, and stand in the gap before me

for the land, that I should not destroy it: but I found none."

The gap is the space that is currently open, but when it's filled, it makes for a seamless process for the ground or things to connect without interruption. I understand that services have spaces that need to be filled, and prayer is the perfect tool to use. My charge is to not use it as secondary but as a primary place. Be intentional with the intercessors and include them in the initial planning so that glory can be totally released and fill all space and time.

Our role as prayer leaders is for us is to stand and proclaim.
Isaiah 12:4 AMP SAYS "Give thanks to the Lord, call on His name [in prayer]. Make His deeds known among the peoples [of the earth]; Proclaim [to them] that His name is exalted!"

Call on the name of The Lord, and Proclaim that His name is Exalted, I love that because His name covers everything.

As prayer leaders, we should have so much meat of the word during our time of prayer and intercession that it's easy for us to relate to the people. We should release scriptures like this and more that will saturate the room and engage the people to come on this journey with us.

Our heavenly language engages us because we are being stirred in our spirit man. However, during the leading of prayer, we should encourage those who are filled with the evidence of tongues to join us. We are to encourage those who are not yet filled to praise in English, pray in English, clap, wave, shout, rock, do something that contributes to the atmosphere.

Leading the service in prayer is to unify the house. It is not time for the prayer leader to show off their new vocabulary words, their fancy tongues, their modulations, and vocal style rifts and runs. The prayer is to bring focus to the presence of God, the cause of the gathering, and the release of Heaven down to the earth. It is a prophetic moment where we speak to the atmosphere and share with our God what we desire for Him to do and what we desire to receive.

Sport teams warm up before fully engaging in their practices for games. Let's look at what it takes players in football and basketball to do while practicing their sport.

Football Practice (www.football-tutorials.com)
• Warm-up & Stretching.

- Review of New Team Plays and/or Conditioning.
- Individual Techniques by Position.
- Special Teams.
- Group Work.
- Game Preparation and Team Drills.
- Cool-Down.

Basketball Practice (www.topendsports.com)
- A slow jog (a lap or two of an oval, or if inside a few laps of the gym)
- 15 minutes of stretching - involving static stretches (quads, hamstrings, calves, torso, shoulders) followed by dynamic stretches (arm circles and swings, leg swings).
- Runs up and down along the side of the court. Running forwards and backwards, side shuffles, leg crossovers.
- 5 × 30m length runs (increase from 50% effort to maximal sprint).
- 5 x 10m out and back short sprints
- 5 zigzag runs (75% effort).
- Basketball drills such as dribbling and shooting.

Football and Basketball are two sports that are high energy, high impact, and highly aggressive towards their opponents. These sports operate at rapid speeds, therefore causing the players to prepare themselves for longevity to endure the entirety of the game. Although not every player is assigned to play the entire game, it is still the responsibility for them to train as if they were. Training for all players is tailored to their respective sport and is the responsibility of each player to adhere to said training, strength, sculpting etc.

Reviewing the list of both sports, I see progression in how they prepare but one sticks out to me over the other. Football practice begins with warm-up and stretching, while basketball practice begins with a slow jog then stretching. It's interesting how both sports begin with a warm-up, granting them time to be centered and focus on stretching parts of the body BEFORE entering the fullness of the game. The warm-up is designed to prepare the body, breathing, movement and prevent possible injuries from occurring.

If the players showed up on the field or court without a proper warm-up and began playing the game, each player would subject themselves to a lack of endurance, stamina, and potential physical harm.

Let's go a little further; when attending Zumba or any group fitness class, the instructor spends time warming up the attendees for a good period of time. Why does he/she do that? The simple answer is if the instructor starts out with movements at a rapid pace and the class is set to be 90 mins, those who attend will not last longer than 15mins or so. Fitness classes are designed for physical endurance, strengthening, toning, and pushing one beyond their normal limits.

Prayer is the same way, whether leading openly or privately. Warm up in prayer! Take your time! Enjoy the entry point, and in time, you will excel to a place where you can move quicker.

As prayer leaders, we must greet the people, acknowledge them, and engage with them as we prepare to go on a journey in the spirit realm. I would not like if a stranger walks up to me and the first words he/she says is "follow me." Well, no, we have not been introduced, and I have no clue where you are going, neither do I know where you are taking me. Prayer is the same way. We as believers understand God and prayer, but there is a set man or woman of God that is standing in a place to take me somewhere in the spirit. Where are we going? What are we doing?

If there is no connection with the people, they will disconnect and fully disengage. The people will get on the ride and fall off if you do not properly coach them along the way.

4 HOW TO BUILD AN EFFECTIVE PRAYER TEAM
(WHY EVERY SENIOR PASTOR NEEDS ONE)

Jeremiah 3:15 KJV "And I will give you pastors according to mine heart, which shall feed you with knowledge and understanding.

A message for our Senior Pastors from a faithful In-house Intercessor.

Having served in church my entire life, from childhood until now, I firmly believe that senior Pastors are directly appointed by God to lead His people to a lifestyle of righteousness and holiness through the word of God. As a young man, I had an aspiration to be a pastor because of my deep love for the church- I wanted to be there all day, every day. However, after seeing some of the truth behind leading God's people, that desire slowly faded away until, unexpectedly, I found myself becoming one anyway.

Pastors, one of the primary reasons we cast vision to those who follow our lead is for them to embrace, embody and be empowered to fulfill that vision. Oftentimes, I've witnessed pastors casting vision for the year, and the initial response from the people may exemplify excitement. However, fast forward three months, and that excitement has dwindled. Six months later, it's nearly nonexistent, and there has been no proof, or manifestation. This can leave the church possibly disconnected and sometimes leads the leader to question whether what was released to the people is still in alignment with God's will, causing frustration with mankind. It's a challenge that some fail to address with those they lead. Vision takes a community of committed believers who are like-minded and willing to press into the journey of fulfillment. God speaks to the leaders yes, but when you stated that this is the place God assigned you to be a part of and help build, then YOU TOO are responsible for fulfilling this charge.

I firmly believe that the weight of the ministry SHOULD rest on the shoulders of the intercessors. Here is why: as vision is cast by the senior leader(s), the first to pick up the vision are the intercessors. Why is that you ask? Simply because we take the vision, write out the vision, map out the vision, and pray it through in parts. As the vision is consistently covered in prayer by a team of intercessors, the manifestation of it shall be released in the timing of

God. Intercessors are not just to pray it through until it manifests but also praying for its sustainability.

Every church should have teams of intercessors to pray for the following:

❖ Senior leader(s) along with first family (Senior pastor and family)
❖ The church and vision of the house
❖ Senior leader(s)personal ministries and businesses (if applicable)
❖ Finances and much more....

In most churches, there are teams assigned to execute various needs in the house. For example:

- Band is comprised of musicians who are skilled to play the sound in and of the house.
- Singers are comprised of individuals who are skilled to sing the sound in and of the house.
- Dancers are comprised of individuals who are skilled to release movements in the house.
- Finance teams handle the tithes, offering, and seed sowing etc.

While there are many more teams that could be listed, one that often seems to be overlooked, mismanaged, or underdeveloped if implemented at all, in the church are the intercessors. Intercessors have been stigmatized as a group of "deep" saints who can pray heaven down, and many people in the church run to them for answers, encouragement, and to help pray for them because they some don't want to pray themselves. Unfortunately, intercessors in the church have sometimes been reduced to a favorite group of people who can shout and scream in prayer, quote numerous scriptures, and have a voice tone that represents a form of "power," but may lack good character or integrity. Oh, I can go on and on about some of these Holy ghost gangs we have called "Intercessory prayer teams".

Nevertheless, intercessory prayer teams are essential in local churches because those who understand the call to intercession are driven solely by the burden of prayer. True intercessors, when connected with like-minded individuals, seek the face of the Lord, stand before the courts of heaven, and cry out day and night until breakthrough occurs in the ministry. They stay on their posts to protect and guard the gates of the house, the senior leader(s), and their families, and will cover the vision at all costs.

Senior Pastors, we need intercessory prayer teams! Yes, we love the music, singing, dancing, and all other areas of ministry in our house but we need a strong army of intercessors! When the enemy

knows intercessors are present, he flees.
Intercessors have the power of God and will ensure
and enforce coverage over everything and everyone
in the house. An intercessor sees the enemy from
afar and sounds the alarm. An intercessor will see
the enemy trying to attack our senior pastor(s) while
they are preaching and suit up from their seat to
pray and cover him/her. Intercessors are dangerous
species who will not allow the plots of the enemy to
take dominion in our camps. NO! We will stand up
and fight until victory is manifested.

Allow me to share something personal that I've
learned from being an intercessor under a senior
pastor and now as a senior pastor myself.

The time I spent in prayer with the Lord was always
intentional. I didn't pray to God to get a
microphone on the platform for public prayer; my
goal was to always delve into the heart of God and
understand His mind. I would always say to myself,
if I want to be an effective, expressive, and clear in
my delivery intercessor that doesn't stammer over
my words or use "space filling words" repeatedly,
then I need to really train myself in prayer. The best
way to start doing so was for me to cover those in
authority. I loved my church and my leaders. The
thought of anything happening to them from the
enemy's camp as a direct assault wasn't going to

occur on my watch. I knew that if my leaders were attacked and went down, I would likely be the next target. My covering kept me protected.

 My covering is what keeps me covered. You will catch that later. If your covering cannot cover you, then you become UNCOVERED AND EXPOSED in a sense.

Let me give you a clearer example; the purpose of the roof is to cover the house. If the roof is removed from the house, everything in it will be exposed and open for anything to come in. The roof is the sealant and protector. Senior pastors are that for the church.

Here's the truth: the greater the weight of glory on a ministry, the greater the need for intercessors. Pastors leading Apostolic and Prophetic houses for example, need to have intercessors that can push and plow in the atmosphere. Pastors who are deliverance centers and revival hubs, require strong intercessors who can navigate and sustain the spiritual atmosphere. Pastors need intercessors!!!!!

There were times when I would come to my church when no one else was there, laboring in prayer and intercession for the house. I would touch every chair, walk the hallways, and pray in the bathrooms and offices because I wanted the glory of God to remain in the house. This wasn't an invitation extended to me by senior leadership, I would call them and ask if I could do so. Eventually, I started asking other intercessors during our weekly prayer meetings, to cover certain parts of the building so we can actively target specific prayers for a specific response from heaven.

Now, as a senior pastor, I understand the value of those years spent in prayer. The church I now pastor along with my wife, has a group of intercessors who pray for us consistently. Every day they send messages, scriptures, and cover our assignments in prayer. We both feel protected and covered by these individuals which gives us the strength to keep moving forward.

Pastors, from one who understands both roles, I urge you to identify a group of at least 3-5 individuals in your church who have your heart and spirit, love the Lord, and are willing to devote themselves to prayer and intercession. Train and equip them to cover the vision of the house, the structure of the house, the finances of the house, the first family, and so much more.

God has anointed me with the gift, skill, and expertise to help develop and train intercessors for the house of God. Prayer Agents is committed to helping those who respond to the call of prayer, providing them with the tools they need to apply in their respective ministries. Our goal is to alleviate the pressure on pastors to produce results and allow them to focus on casting vision and watching it manifest and grow.

So, how do you build a team of intercessors? Recognize the need for intercession day and night, identify those in the house who have the heart of the ministry, and provide opportunities for prayer services and connections with prayer experts to equip them for the task.

5 HOW TO COVER SENIOR LEADERSHIP

As a child, most of my friends were always older than me. I realized that I could only connect to those who were of a mature stature because I would hear repeatedly that I acted older than my age. I found myself being a kid who always respected my elders and honored adults. So much so that I was rarely excluded from adult conversations and was sometimes included to provide my thoughts depending on the topic. I recall being 12 old, and my best friend was about 45 years old at the time. Yes, I said it, 45 years old. She and I would talk on the phone for hours, and she loved my family. It was because of this woman that I took my first driving test, and she gave me my first car. She was such an amazing woman of God. I was able to have intellectual conversations about the church, prayer, the Bible and so much more because I gravitated towards older saints in the church, and they became my friends in my young eyes.

Many might find this unusual and wonder what it has to do with covering senior leadership. Glad you asked me this question. Here is the deal, because I was so advanced as a child, youth, teen and young adult, my assignment has always been to assist executive (top tier) leaders.

In every job I've had, I was close to the CEO or whoever was closest to the highest in operations. Over the years, God has groomed me to understand the ins and outs of leading corporations and various systems in the world while being connected to the top leader. I was entrusted to work alongside or right underneath some powerful leaders, and God made my name great.

I would ask God sometimes, why am I here in this capacity and it wasn't until I recognized that I am to learn what it is like to be in that position so I can be an effective intercessor with accurate intel to cover in prayer.

Looking at our churches, we tend to believe that our senior pastors are like Marvel or DC comic heroes. It is perceived as if senior leaders do have not a care in the world and do not need our prayers. This is the biggest lie the enemy could ever tell the church. I wanted to take time to really expound upon why our intercessors and prayer warriors need to cover senior leadership.

Why is covering Senior Leadership Important?
What attacks them, attacks you!
What distracts them, can distract you!
What takes from them, takes from you!

7 Areas to cover in prayer for Senior Leader(s)
4.   Health (Physical, mental, spiritual, emotional)
James 5:14-15 KJV
14 Is any sick among you? let him call for the elders
of the church; and let them pray over him,
anointing him with oil in the name of the Lord:
15 And the prayer of faith shall save the sick, and
the Lord shall raise him up; and if he have
committed sins, they shall be forgiven him.

2.   Gifts (creativity , staying focused on the usage of respective gifts)
Colossians 3:23-24 NIV
Whatever you do, work at it with all your heart, as
working for the Lord, not for human masters, 24
since you know that you will receive an inheritance
from the Lord as a reward. It is the Lord Christ you
are serving.

3.   Finances
Genesis 1:28-29 KJV
 And God blessed them, and God said unto them,
Be fruitful, and multiply, and replenish the earth,

and subdue it: and have dominion over the fish of the sea, and over the fowl of the air, and over every living thing that moveth upon the earth.

29 And God said, Behold, I have given you every herb bearing seed, which is upon the face of all the earth, and every tree, in the which is the fruit of a tree yielding seed; to you it shall be for meat.

4.   Home (children, pets, marriages, all connected to first family as well as properties)

Isaiah 32:18 KJV
And my people shall dwell in a peaceable habitation, and in sure dwellings, and in quiet resting places;

5.   Business (all business affairs connected to them present and future)

Proverbs 16:3 KJV
Commit thy works unto the Lord, and thy thoughts shall be established.

6.   Vision (purpose, destiny, for the house as a whole)
I Samuel 3:19 AMP
19 Now Samuel grew; and the Lord was with him and He let none of his words [c]fail [to be fulfilled].

7.   <u>Spirit (make intercession for them spiritually)</u>
Ephesians 3:16 AMP
May He grant you out of the riches of His glory, to
be strengthened and spiritually energized with
power through His Spirit in your inner self,
[indwelling your innermost being and personality],

<u>Effective Prayer/Intercession Solutions for senior
leadership</u>
Close up every breach- (leave nothing open or
exposed)
2 Kings 12: 5b they shall repair any breach in the
house of the Lord, wherever a breach is found."

<u>Make up the hedge-Ezekiel 22:30 KJV</u>
And I sought for a man among them, that should
make up the hedge, and stand in the gap before me
for the land, that I should not destroy it: but I
found none.

<u>Never leave them uncovered Isaiah 59:16 KJV</u>
And he saw that there was no man, and wondered
that there was no intercessor: therefore his arm
brought salvation unto him; and his righteousness,
it sustained him.

Report what you see Ezekiel 3:17 KJV

Son of man, I have made thee a watchman unto the house of Israel: therefore hear the word at my mouth, and give them warning from me.

Supernatural deliverance (Acts 12:5,11)

Peter therefore was kept in prison: but prayer was made without ceasing of the church unto God for him.

And when Peter was come to himself, he said, Now I know of a surety, that the Lord hath sent his angel, and hath delivered me out of the hand of Herod, and from all the expectation of the people of the Jews.

Prayer/Intercession Template for Prayer Agents covering leaders.

- ❖ Identify the Focus area/Topic.
- ❖ What is the expected outcome of the prayer?
- ❖ What are some of the oppositions concerning this topic? Current or future?
- ❖ Locate scriptures associated with the topic, expected outcome and oppositions.
- ❖ Pray in direct symmetry of this as often as God intends.

Things to remember Prayer Agents when covering Senior Leader(s)

❖ Carry the burden of prayer and intercession for the leader in a selfless manner.

❖ Remember, YOU matter so move in accordance with the spirit of God. It shall be YOUR strength.

❖ Build yourself up in prayer and intercession.

❖ Carry and deliver the assignment until the appointed time of release.

❖ Assignments shift, DO NOT STAY THERE TOO LONG.

6 HOW TO ADMINISTER ALTAR PRAYER

Altar prayer practices vary among churches and para-ministries, but they all have one thing in common: the altar itself. The altar serves as the place of sacrifice and offering, where we encounter the presence of God. As we surrender ourselves to Him, there is an exchange that occurs at the altar. Whatever is removed from us is replaced with things of God that will deepen our connection with Him.

In this chapter, I would like to focus on a few best practices of my own that I have found beneficial in administering altar prayer effectively. When souls come to the altar, it is either voluntarily, involuntarily, or by invitation. In other words, they come to the altar because they want to, they have to, or have been summoned or commissioned to come.

The altar is where we experience significant live events such as marriages, baby dedications, soul dedications, and funerals. Therefore, it is a sacred place that requires that us as intercessors to be mindful of our language, physical points of contact, voice tone, volume and much more. Otherwise, we risk exposing our weaknesses as "presented experts." OH yeah, this may offend many people, but we have to go there.

Altar work is not for the faint at heart, those wanting to be seen, the undelivered, or spiritually unprepared. As spirits are being released, they require a skilled midwife in healing and deliverance to properly aid them to the place of freedom. We say this a lot in the church that "spirits transfer" and I do believe this is VERY true. However, as intercessors, we must grasp what transpires at the altar and assert our authority in that space until individuals break through.

Let's talk a little more on how to properly handle the souls at the altar. I have been an altar worker for many years, and I have seen successes and failures. Honestly, most of my life I have experienced the altar being mishandled by altar workers. I have seen intercessors who wanted to operate in "the power" so greatly that they were yelling, hollering, and pushing people to the floor yielding no spiritual impact. I have seen souls crying out and wanting to be free and the intercessor was praying from their soulish realm but not in tune with the heart cry of the soul. There were also instances where intercessors failed to maintain alignment with individuals seeking deliverance, leaving them vulnerable and unsupported throughout the process. I have seen A LOT!!!!!!!!!!!

Prayer Agents, we are altar working experts who will stand firm in the word of God to pull His people out of bondage into the place of God-ordained freedom. How can we do so? I am so glad you asked. Here are 9 recommended ways administer altar prayer effectively.

1. Connect with God's Spirit: As the souls are approaching the altar, take a minute to align yourself with the spirit of God, recognizing that all men deserve freedom. This is not the time to judge or pry as to why the souls are at the altar, but for God to reveal to you through His mysteries what each soul needs.

2. Discern Your Assignment: Scan the room and ask God which souls you are graced to pray for. Everyone at the altar MAY NOT BE within your assigned capacity, so seek divine direction before approaching anyone.

3. Seek God's Guidance: Once you identify your assigned soul, begin to ask the Lord what he/she stands in need of. This will help to stir your spirit and align with God's will for the soul you're assigned to pray for.)

4. <u>Follow the Spirit's Lead:</u> When approaching your soul, be led by the spirit. Not every approach requires laying hands on their head or yelling; allow yourself to flow in the Spirit and speak what God reveals.

5. <u>Coach the Soul Through the Process</u>: While praying and interceding coach the soul through the journey. Do not spend time prophesying to them if that's not what God is saying. Intercede and pray them through and coach them by saying words of a midwife.

Note: Many times, I will say things like, "you got this", "you're almost there", "come on and tell God you're letting it go", or things that encourages the soul to lead the way to their own freedom. Support the soul to the point of deliverance.

6. <u>Remain vigilant:</u> Keep your eyes open while praying and interceding at the altar, staying aware of your surroundings. If demonic manifestations occur, recognize the signs and know how to address them. The only way eyes should be closed is if you have 2-3 intercessors with you and they are watching and praying.

7. <u>Pray Until Completion</u>: Intercede and pray until you know the soul have reached their point of completion. DO NOT WRESTLE long at the altar for someone who does not want freedom and not willing to commit to the process. You cannot want it more than them.

8. <u>Be honest and Direct</u>: Be honest at the altar with your soul. Ask them, if needed, do you want freedom? Are you wanting to make a change? Remember Prayer Agent, you are the coach, and the soul is the player. We are the experts!

9. <u>Flow as a Prophetic Intercessor</u>- Be the prophet while being the intercessor. Meaning you will see, hear, and sense things about the soul and God will allow you to share. However, flow with God in knowing what to share and how to share it. Some things must be said to break the yoke and expose the spirit that's hijacking them.

I want to add this as a bonus: Use wisdom while using the word of God. Do not pray from experiences of your own but only release the word of God that is necessary for that person to connect with for their own deliverance.

Again, these are 9 ways that I recommend and there are many more, but we want to be effective altar workers. These methods aim to make altar workers effective and impactful in their ministry of prayer and intercession. The effectual, fervent prayers of a righteous man availeth much-James 5:16b. That's that what we need at the altar. Experts in the spirit of God who can discern, speak with boldness and confidence and will be midwives to someone in need of deliverance

7 HOW TO RELEASE PROPHETIC INTERCESSION

Hosea 12:10 GW "I spoke to the prophets and gave them many visions. I taught lessons through the prophets.

V. 13 "The Lord used a prophet to bring the people of Israel out of Egypt. He used a prophet to take care of them.

The prophetic anointing is very special. The prophets are dear to the heart of God because they convey His direct messages to His people. What I truly enjoy about the prophetic is, there are no boundaries or discrimination to who can benefit from the prophetic. In other words, whoever God has a word for whether saved or sinner, when He has something to say, He says it through an obedient vessel.

Despite the perversion and skepticism surrounding the prophetic in our generation, God remains faithful to His word and continues to speak through obedient vessels. Look at this scripture: Amos 3:7 GW "Certainly, the Almighty Lord doesn't do anything unless he ⌊first⌋ reveals his secret to his servants the prophets.

Hear me and hear me clearly, prophets are nothing but intercessors. Yes, I said it, prophets are intercessors and the two work together. When we pray, we receive information from the Lord and that same information is then released to the people. To get clarity on a word from God, you pray. If you need to hear a word from God, you pray.

Now, let's talk about how the prophet and intercessor are married (in my own words) which is called "Prophetic Intercession". This is when you take information received from the spirit of God, research it as needed, and then begin to pray it through. During the time of prayer and intercession, the topic, target, or situation is therefore made more clearer as you continue to cry out.

Allow me to share a personal experience to illustrate the power of prophetic intercession. I was scheduled to pray for a sister of mine, live recording. The title of the recording was "Birth It". As I was preparing to minister, my hearts cry unto God was what do I pray. The only direction the Lord gave me was to search for scriptures on birthing. I located about six scriptures on the topic of birthing and began to practice praying them through. Yes, I practice my prayers because I for one would not like to hold a phone or iPad in my hand while going before God in prayer. In order for me to be hands free, I take the time to familiarize myself with scriptures and get them in my spirit and He will cause me to remember where they are located.

Moments before I was getting ready to mount the stage to pray, the Holy Spirit said to pray for women who had abortions and miscarriages and command them to receive forgiveness from shame and embarrassment. I heard those words and immediately I became afraid. I had never prayed along those lines before publicly and I did not want to offend anyone. It was tough!!!! I said God are you sure? He said yes, someone listening needs to know I have forgiven them and that I have not cursed their wombs because of an abortion or miscarriage.

As I begin to pray on the microphone every scripture I studied, the Lord did not allow me to release all six but only about 2-3 of them. He then shifted me to Hannah in 1 Samuel chapter 1 and said to pray against barren wombs and command the spirit of Peninnah that's been tormenting Hannah to die. Seconds later, the prayer shifted to women who had abortions and miscarriages. From there I had to keep going and I'm hearing the crowd get louder and louder in praise with more intensity as I continued to pray and intercede.

Once the prayer ended, my sister began to share her testimony of battling shame due to an abortion and did an altar call for women who dealt with infertility issues. My God. The power of God came into the room and women who came to the altar received hope, inspiration, and restoration from God our Father.

Intercessors don't be afraid to follow God in the realm of the prophetic. We hear God as we pray, and He only reveals to us what He desires for the people to know IN PRAYER! I love prophetic intercession because it allows you to declare, decree, admit, acknowledge, speak to, break off, shift, ascend and much more over people, places, and things. It's never one sided! It's a form of prayer that transcends boundaries and dimensions, allowing us to access deeper realms of God's presence and authority. I really feel God as I'm typing this!!!!!

The prophets are sought after by jezebel to kill the sound and the message that we possess but we shall never be stopped. Rise up Prophetic Intercessor and say what the Lord has commanded!

8 HOW TO STRUCTURE A CORPORATE SHUT-IN

Growing up in COGIC (Church of God In Christ), prayer shut-ins were a normal part of church attendance. I mean, we had them on Sundays, midweek, or whenever it was necessary for the saints to gather in one room to pray. I was birthed in the era of the church where once the shut-in started, the doors were locked and did not open until we ended. We did not have musicians playing during our time of prayer and rarely did we have someone leading corporate prayer. As a child, we were not allowed to bring our toys, games, books, or anything like that from the house. The children were treated like adults in prayer shut-ins as we all came into the room with one mind and one spirit and that was to seek the face of the Lord. Everyone was responsible for getting to God and hearing from God in their own way.

I was the kid who never fussed or complained about being in prayer because I enjoyed every minute of it. Now, I am going to reveal a secret to you prayer agents and I need to make sure you keep this to yourself. You ready? I used to skip school at times to attend prayer shut ins. Yep, I was that kind of kid. It was something about being in the presence of God through prayer that excited me, stirred me up and made me feel so close to the Lord.

Nowadays, prayer shut-ins have faded to a silent place. Not every ministry has removed them, but it's been very scarce as time has come along. We need musicians to play during prayer. We need a prayer leader the entire time. We need dictionaries and encyclopedias if we are coming to a prayer gathering or form of a shut-in. Our children don't have patience or stamina to endure an hour of prayer without their phones, tablets, and devices. Well, not just our children, but our adults need something entertaining to keep them engaged during prayer as well. The sound of saints praying and crying out has a time limit in certain atmospheres because we only want God for a period of time. It's quite disheartening that shut-ins are the place of intimacy with God, but we still need aid and assistance to get us to God. There are some who would attend a shut in and would be so lost on where to start they would either not engage or not stay in the room.

The Lord has been pressing upon me to go back to prayer shut-ins where the focus is based upon

Psalms 91:1: GW Whoever lives under the shelter of the Most High, will remain in the shadow of the Almighty.

I love this translation and the terminology that says "lives" and "remain". These words give language for shut-ins that says for hours I am going to live in this place of your presence and when this intimate time is over, my spirit will forever remain in your presence. Wow!

In 2023, I hosted 11 months of training, impartation and activation for the intercessors called "The Gathering of Intercessors". The final month we spent 3 days together to seal up what God had been speaking to us all year long. While in prayer two months before the final gathering, the Lord spoke to me and said you are going to have a 24-hour shut in. I was shocked because I had never attended a 24-hour shut-in, and now I'm hosting one. It was at that moment I had to seek the face of God concerning this plan of action. How do we sustain the spirit of God for 24 consecutive hours? The goal was not for me to say "Aye God, I did what you said and we lasted 24 hours, whoo hooo"!. The goal was for each prayer hour to be intentional and progressive. The goal was for the people to want to remain in the house the entire time and if they did have to leave, they would be able to come back and ascend from where they left off.

I reached out to my brothers and sisters in Christ who were coming to help me plow in prayer and intercession for the entire 24 hours and asked their availability. It was from that place I created a "projected" schedule. In my efforts to help you plan a successful glory-filled shut-in no matter the duration of time, I want to share what worked for me.

24-Hour Prayer Schedule:
- 10:30pm (Doors open to the public)
- 11pm-11:50pm (instrumental soaking)
- 12am-12:50am (Prayer Leader)
- 1:00-1:50am (Prayer Leader)
- 2:00am-2:50am (Prayer Leader)
- 3:00am-4:50am (Worship Leader (song, prayer and prophecy)
- 4:50am-6:00am (instrumental soaking)
- 6:00am-7:50am(Prayer Leader)
- 7:50-9:00am (instrumental soaking)
- 9am-10:50am (Prayer Leader)
- 11am-11:50am (Hour of Worship)
- 12pm-1:50pm (Prayer leader)
- 2:00pm-2:50pm (Instrumental soaking)
- 3pm-4:50 pm (Miracle Hours of Prayer)
- 5pm-6pm (instrumental worship)

- 6pm-7:50pm (Prayer Leader)
- 8pm-8:50pm worship (instrumental soaking)
- 9pm-11pm (Prayer Leader)

The shut-in was comprised of prayer and worship leaders, as well as moments of instrumental soaking music. The goal of our shut-in was for us to pray and seek the Lord, hear from God through the men and women chosen by Him to facilitate during their various timeslots, engage in moments of corporate worship, and then have breaks where we could sit with God individually and listen. The strategy behind placing facilitators in a specific order that would cause a journey of ascension was key. It was imperative that those whom God chose to release the sound of prayer were a part of this journey. I was aware of their strength in prayer and intercession, which also gave me the ability to place them accordingly. I understood who prophetic intercessors were, versus those who were worship leaders, and those who possessed the power of healing and deliverance in their hands etc. I must say the number of attendees ranged from 40-60 the entire 24 hours! The people stayed in the glory, and God was glorified. During the 3pm miracle hour, we saw people get healed from sciatica in the back, pain in the legs, joints that were swollen dissolved and much more. The conclusion of the shut-in from 10pm-11pm was filled with singing the songs of the Lord without a lead on the microphone. The intercessors were singing while the minstrel played on the keyboard.

My advice and strong encouragement for those of you hosting prayer shut ins: Only invite the voices God has chosen to release prayer and intercession, not those whom you like, who are popular, or can draw a crowd. The purpose of the prayer shut-in is for the saints to get on one accord and seek GOD! He is the star! He is what's important!

9 HOW TO FACILITATE A 72 HOUR PRAYER WATCH

December 26th-29th, 2021 The Lord called me to host my first 72-hour prayer assignment with a team of intercessors who worked alongside me with Prayer Agents United. I recall being in prayer a week prior, and the Lord said the only way to hear what I am saying to the church is to consistently seek me over a period of days. I rallied my team together and gave them the word of the Lord and requested their attention to this matter, and all of them graciously submitted to the voice of the Lord.

Our focus was to pray around the 8 prayer watches:
○   6pm-9pm-First Watch
○   9pm-12am-Second Watch
○   12am-3am-Third Watch
○   3am-6am-Fourth Watch
○   6am-9am-Fifth Watch
○   9am-12pm-Sixth Watch
○   12pm-3pm-Seventh Watch
○   3pm-6pm-Eighth Watch

A team of 21 people came together in prayer

consecutive for 72 hours, each having one-two hours a day of prayer to hear the Lord speak. Upon reading every message from the intercessors, the voice of the Lord was so clear in what He was looking for us to target in prayer. 2022 was a year to pray for children, His church, judgment and much more. The blessing of our submission and obedience to this prayer was that it was individually done per hour while keeping the spirit of unity as a team focused on seeking God. We covered the earth, the world, and the people for 72 consecutive hours. We did not speak to one another on the phone or anything. We each prayed our hour, and all the words from God came directly to me via email and text message.

My heart began to truly cry out to God in deep intercession as every hour intensified and His voice was becoming more stronger to each of us.

Dear Prayer Agent, I strongly encourage you to connect with like-minded individuals who are willing to embark on a journey of seeking God over an extended period. Find people who are up for a similar challenge.

I will say this, during those three days, we noticed a decrease in crime reported by the media, and an increase in peace across our various regions. Our team comprised of individuals from Tennessee, Kentucky, California, Illinois, and Indiana. Despite being from different regions and operating on different timeframes, we remained synchronized in the spirit of God, united in our pursuit to seek Him.

The Lord spoke to us during this time, addressing some things globally, regionally, and personally. Take the charge Prayer Agents! There is so much to pray and intercede for as we impact the world, the earth, and its people.

10 THE COMMITTED PRAYER AGENT

I wanted to conclude PT. 1 of Prayer Agents manual with this topic to support those of you who are committed to this life of prayer and intercession. Throughout this manual, I have shared some of my best practices, personal encounters, and revelations from the spirit of God concerning prayer. There are indeed benefits to being committed to God in prayer and interceding for others. I say this all the time, "Once a son, always a son."

My wife created a shirt for me that I proudly especially when I minister. It's called "Intercessors Nutrition facts," similar to what you would see on the back of food packaging.

Here is what is says:

Serving Size: 1 Kingdom Kid

Creativity: 1200%

Authenticity: 200%

Passion: 200%

Bible Knowledge: OVERDOSED

Prayer: 1000%

Sleep: 0%

*Daily values may be higher or lower depending on the motivation and mood.

My wife created these figures and percentages, and she was spot-on. We decided to patent and trademark this information and add it to our clothing line so that every Prayer Agent can wear their assignment proudly.

I wanted to make mention of this to encourage you all regarding your assignment to pray and intercede. As one who has been true to this assignment, I can relate to the feeling of questioning if it's all worth it. Asking yourself, "Am I beneficial to the call of prayer?"

Once you have given and poured so much, it may feel like you're not growing in God. You may ask yourself questions like "Is my prayer and intercession life bearing any fruit?"

I want to close with an encounter that occurred with me in the last year. When I wrote Prayer Agents book back in 2020, I shared that as I completed the book, I went through divorce. As a result, I had to find myself back to praying and seeking God, which was incredibly difficult. I went through seasons of feeling hurt, ashamed, and I really do not know how to recover from it. Prayer Agents publication helped me in more ways than one. I regained a new strength in the community of intercessors that boosted my strength and courage to keep the faith and keep plowing in prayer.

As I continued serving in my church, I didn't know what was ahead for me. I didn't know what God had planned, but I knew that I needed to continue in prayer and intercession for my spiritual parents, my church family, and other assignments. I found myself still coming to the church when no one was there and praying in the sanctuary for about an hour or so. I found myself hearing from God in different ways, and it took intercession to open my heart to again.

The divorce broke me down so badly that I felt like I lost my lifeline to prayer. My heart was closed to the point where hope for an opening was nonexistent. One day in prayer, I asked God to detox my heart from bitterness concerning love and, if it is His Will for me to marry, then give me an Adam and Eve experience. To present my wife to me after me I had been in a deep sleep, removing my rib from me. I'll share more on this story in another book, but needless to say, I was presented my Eve, and I got married the second time around to a beautiful, gorgeous Queen.

My "Eve" was not a resident of my hometown of Chicago, IL which meant it was time for me to completely relocate my life from Chicago to Houston in a matter of months. Again, the details of this story will be shared in another book.

For 14 years, I served in a ministry where my heart for prayer and intercession was loud and visible.

When I left my home church, it took me through grievances that I could not imagine. But, let me tell you the benefits of being a committed son.

I returned to my home church about 2 months after I got married just to visit. The service was about to begin, and my spiritual father asked me to pray in the service. I was like, "Oh Lord, no way, what am I going to pray?"

The moment I mounted the stage, I opened my mouth and allowed the Holy Spirit to pray through me, and it shifted the room.

The funny thing is my spiritual father was not in the room during the time of my prayer. As I was releasing prayer, the word "revival" came out my mouth, and we labored there praising and shouting for revival to hit the room.

Moments later my spiritual father got up to preach and out of his mouth goes the word "revival". He began to command revival in the room. We talked after church, and some members of the church, as well as me, shared with him those were words that came out in prayer earlier in the service. The only thing I said to myself again was "once a son, always a son". The connection never leaves you! Once you're connected and have been imparted into, you will see that it will always come out.

Here is my charge to senior pastors, senior leaders and those who serve in ministry. Your connection in prayer and intercession is valuable not just for you but those you are assigned to. We need one another more than we sometimes express. It was awesome to know that although I served in a ministry for 14 years and became a senior pastor of my current church, that when I go home, I still flow and function from the deposits I had received. I can be like the prodigal son, and when I get home, my father welcomes me with the robe and a ring along with gifts and a celebration because we are connected forever.

Pastors, we need those devoted prayer warriors that will cry aloud in our sanctuaries and cover us in prayer. Prayer Agents, you need to be under coverings who value and appreciate your pour. We are not enemies in this kingdom, but we are allies together aiming for glory to be released in all we do and everywhere we go.

CHARGE TO THE INTERCESSORS (UNDERSTANDING YOUR GRACE AS A PRAYER AGENT)

Intercession without information is not effective or impactful.

Imagine a football game being played on the field. Now, picture someone who has never shown up to practice, has little to no knowledge of how to play the game, and has never watched a game before. This person arrives at the field as the game is starting or already in full operation, dressed in regular attire because they're unsure of what to wear. They step onto the field without selecting a team, seeing a coach, or seeking counsel. They approach the field simply because they want to play.

As they stand on the field, the ball comes in their direction, and they reach up to grab it, taking off running. However, other players are not coming after them because it's startling how they're not dressed in uniform, yet they're on the field playing with them and running with the very thing that's the nucleus of the game—the football. This person runs fast and scores a touchdown, but it's only because they ran to the end of the field unknowledgeable about who they just scored a point for. They don't realize that reaching the field goal was pointless because they were not authorized to play in the first place.

All of this was a waste of time, attention, energy, confusion, and frustration to those players who have worked hard in practice, came dressed to play, and aimed to defeat opponents. Yet, this person saw it as an opportunity.

Intercessors MUST have information about the game, region, territory, teammates, opponents so that when approaching the field for battle, it's a fair game. Intercessors NEVER lose with having vital information on the field. It defeats their opposing teams EVERY TIME!

Prayer releases information.
Intercession applies information.
Prophetic is birthed and seals up the information.

Prophetic intercession shifts the directions BASED upon information revealed. Prayer will give you the word of prophecy. If you pray, you will get a word. As you use the word in intercession, it becomes more detailed and clearer as you release and actively engage.

The prophetic gives the information for the vessel's next steps indicating what to expect, what is required, and what is sustainable.

Father in the name of Jesus, I pray for your senior leaders and your Prayer Agents who have taken out time to read this manual and I declare that new language and a fresh pour will be open them in the name of Jesus. Father just as your eyes are everywhere looking on good and evil according to Proverbs 15:3, I pray that the eyes of the leaders are fixated on the intercessors and the intercessors eyes on the leaders and we both are guided in faith by the spirit of God.

Father, I ask that we now use these tools from this manual and apply them in our cities, homes, nations and all regions. I decree and declare that God of angel's armies be with us and protect us. Let us speak the language of the kingdom and cause there to be a collision between heaven and earth. Father, let us build effective teams, and began to dominate our cities with prayer shut-ins where we cry out until we get heaven to respond.

Father, I pray for the weary intercessor and those who lost heart and I declare that because of this manual, this has caused a spiritual awakening and a stirring in their spirit IN THE NAME OF JESUS.

www.ingramcontent.com/pod-product-compliance
Lightning Source LLC
Chambersburg PA
CBHW052137090426
42741CB00009B/2121